WHEN THE SKY BURNED RED

A Memoir of the Biafran War

Alexander Iloka Rajis

Staten House Press
New York, New York

ISBN: 979-8-90417-456-9

Published by Staten House Press
New York, New York

DEDICATION

For those who endured the Biafran War,
and for those whose lives were lost
to hunger, violence, and displacement.

AUTHOR'S NOTE

This memoir recounts lived experience during the Biafran War (1967–1970). While the documented anti-Igbo pogroms of 1966 preceded the formal outbreak of war, this narrative opens within the war itself, as it was first understood and lived by a child.

Memories of earlier violence surface later in the text, not as background, but as part of a continuum in which mass violence against civilians functioned as a tool of terror and coercion.

This work is offered as witness and remembrance rather than as a comprehensive political or military history.

TABLE OF CONTENTS

PART I — WAR

PART I — WAR

The war was already part of our lives before I understood what a war was.

I was fifteen then, the eldest of ten siblings, old enough to sense danger and young enough to still believe the world could be repaired. Hunger arrived first—quietly, disguised as smaller meals and longer waits. Then came fear, unspoken but everywhere. The sound of aircraft overhead taught us new rules: when to run, when to lie still, when to pretend the sky did not matter. Childhood did not end in a single moment. It was dismantled, piece by piece.

We learned to read the sky the way others read clocks. The pitch of an engine told us whether to scatter or stay low. Even silence had meaning. It could be safety, or it could be the pause before something worse.

I did not yet understand borders or names. I did not know what Biafra meant. I only knew that food was scarce, people moved constantly, and adults spoke in fragments. Radios were guarded. News traveled faster than certainty. The world narrowed to what could be done today.

Bombing was not constant, but it was enough—enough to make sleep fragile, enough to make homes feel temporary, enough to convince us that nowhere was permanent anymore.

People disappeared. Sometimes they returned thinner and quieter. Sometimes they did not return at all. Loss became ordinary, which was perhaps the most frightening thing of all.

Years later I understood that the war did not begin with bombs alone. It began with people being marked, hunted, and driven to flee—long before front lines were drawn.

At the time, I only knew that the sky had turned against us, and that the war had already decided who we were allowed to be.

Hunger did not arrive with an announcement. It came the way weather comes—first as a change in the air, then as a rule nobody could ignore.

At the beginning, adults tried to hide it from us. They spoke of shortages as if patience could bring things back. Meals grew smaller without being named smaller. Water was measured. Kerosene was saved. Nothing was wasted—not because we had become disciplined, but because waste had become dangerous.

The market changed first. It was still noisy, still crowded, still bargaining and laughter that sounded too loud. But tables looked different. Familiar goods vanished. Familiar prices became insults. People learned substitutions, and then learned the substitutions would also disappear. The market did not die. It thinned, like a man losing weight too quickly.

Adults avoided big words. They did not say "famine." They said "we will manage." They did not say "starvation." They said "hard times." But children hear what words are meant to cover. Hunger teaches itself. A body learns the empty time between meals, the dizziness, the quiet the body becomes when it is trying to save itself.

At first I believed hunger was temporary. Later it stopped feeling temporary. It became the background of everything— like dust on the floor. You did not ask when it would end. You asked what could be done today.

We learned small calculations. If you ate now, would there be anything later? If you shared, would the pot become empty sooner? Children learned the math of survival before we learned the math of school.

Sometimes food arrived suddenly and unevenly. Someone would whisper that something was available somewhere, and people moved as if delay itself were a mistake. You could feel the shift before you saw it—the way shoulders turned, the way feet began to hurry.

Even when there was something, there was never enough.

Hunger rearranged people. Mothers stretched meals. Fathers returned with small victories. Neighbors offered water without being asked. Pride became fragile. Care became deliberate.

Later, people would argue about policies and numbers and decisions made far away. Those debates have their place. But hunger, as we lived it, was not a statistic. It was the daily narrowing of possibility.

And it was the knowledge—quiet, learned slowly—that hunger was not only a condition of war. It could be used. It could be directed. It could be made to do work without ever lifting a weapon.

That is what hunger taught me: some forms of violence do not make noise, and the body remembers them long after the mind finds language.

We did not leave because we had chosen a destination. We left because staying had become impossible.

Displacement did not begin with an order. It began with small decisions that felt temporary. Someone said it might be safer elsewhere. Someone else said we would return soon. People gathered what they could carry, not knowing whether they were packing for days or for years.

There were no maps for what we were doing. Roads existed, but certainty did not. Movement itself became the plan.

At first, we traveled in groups that still resembled families. Later, groups broke apart and reformed. People attached themselves to whoever was moving in the same direction. Names mattered less than proximity. Safety became a shared hope rather than a guarantee.

Distance lost meaning. The body measured progress differently now—by thirst, by exhaustion, by the ache that settled into the legs and refused to leave. Children learned to keep moving even when tired, because stopping did not feel safe.

Vehicles appeared and disappeared like favors. A lorry might carry us for a while, then leave us somewhere unfamiliar. Trains came crowded, already full before they stopped, doors opening onto bodies pressed together so tightly there was no room for dignity. People climbed aboard without asking where the train was headed. Direction mattered less than escape.

The landscape blurred. Towns became names spoken without explanation. Memory kept only fragments: a road bending sharply, a tree that offered brief shade, the sound of adults arguing over whether to continue or rest.

Later, measured by people who wanted distances to make sense, parts of our flight would be described in miles— hundreds of miles, as if a number could contain what it meant to walk for days and nights. At the time, it was not miles. It was endurance.

At night, sleep came in pieces. People lay close, not for comfort but for reassurance that no one had disappeared while they were not looking. A child could wake and not recognize where they were, only to realize that recognition itself had become a luxury.

What stayed with me most was the feeling of being unanchored. Home had once been a place you returned to. Now it was something you remembered. Arrival did not bring rest— only another temporary pause.

Later, people would speak of routes and evacuations and population movement. Those words suggest organization. What we lived through felt closer to improvisation: an ongoing response to danger that kept changing its shape.

Displacement taught me that survival is not always heroic. Sometimes it is repetitive. Sometimes it is simply the refusal to stop moving when stopping might mean being found.

By the time we paused long enough to believe we might stay, I had already learned something I would not unlearn: belonging can be interrupted, and once interrupted, it does not easily return.

A house is not a place when it can no longer promise tomorrow.

In the beginning, we still spoke of "home" as if it were fixed. Even after we had moved once, we used the word the way people use a compass—something that points to where you belong. But war makes belonging unstable. It does not only move bodies; it loosens the meaning of places.

We stayed where we could—rooms borrowed from people who had already borrowed them, corners of buildings never meant for living, shelters defined less by walls than by the brief permission to stop. A home became any place where you could lie down without being immediately forced to stand again.

Adults tried to rebuild ordinary life in fragments. They swept. They arranged mats. They cooked when there was something to cook. They spoke in low voices, as if small rituals could persuade the world to behave. But nothing stayed arranged for long. People arrived suddenly. People left suddenly. News traveled through rooms faster than rest.

There were places that felt safe until they didn't. Safety did not always leave with noise. Sometimes it left quietly— through rumor, through a look on someone's face, through a sudden tightening in adult voices. A home could change in one afternoon from shelter to risk.

When the sky was loud, we listened for the movement of others. The world outside entered our rooms even when no one came through the door. The fear came in first, then the decisions. Where can we go? Who can we stay with? What can we carry? Who will be behind?

It is difficult to describe what it does to a child to live in places that keep dissolving. A child needs the stability of repetition: the same doorway, the same street, the same predictable morning. War breaks repetition apart. It teaches you to memorize quickly and to let go even faster.

I began to notice the small signs that a place would not hold. The way adults stopped unpacking. The way bags stayed close. The way people slept wearing the clothes they would need to run. The way a room grew quieter not because it was peaceful but because everyone was listening.

A home is not only walls. It is a promise.

During the war, promises were the first things to burn.

War did not ask a child's permission before changing them.

At first, I still thought of myself as a child. I noticed small things the way children do: a missing game, a friend who did not come back, the way laughter sounded thinner than before. But the war did not allow those losses to remain small. Each absence added weight, until childhood itself began to feel like something we had misplaced.

Adults tried to protect us by controlling what we saw. They sent children away when conversations turned serious. They lowered their voices. They replaced answers with reassurances. But protection has limits in war. Fear moves faster than instructions, and children learn by watching what adults do when they think no one is watching.

I watched faces more closely than before. I learned to recognize the look that meant something was wrong, even when no one said it. I learned that silence could mean danger, and that noise could mean the same thing. I learned that questions were not always welcome, and that knowing when not to ask was a kind of intelligence.

Play did not disappear all at once. It shrank.

Games became shorter. Laughter became careful. Joy required scanning the surroundings first, as if happiness itself needed permission. Even when children played, there was a restlessness underneath, a readiness to stop and move if the world shifted again.

Responsibility arrived early.

Children learned to fetch water, to wait in lines, to keep track of siblings, to stay quiet when told. We learned which roads were safer and which times of day were better for moving. We learned how to make ourselves smaller, not because we wanted to disappear, but because attention had become risky.

I learned to sleep lightly and wake quickly, not because anyone taught me to, but because the body remembers what the mind has not yet named.

There were moments when I felt older than I was, and moments when I felt younger than ever. War compresses time. It asks a child to grow up in some ways while leaving other parts unfinished. I carried both at once: awareness and confusion, caution and longing.

By the time I realized childhood was no longer intact, it had already changed shape. It had narrowed. It had hardened in places. It had learned to carry things it was not designed to hold.

The war did not end childhood in a single moment. It surrounded it, pressed in on it, and slowly made it something else.

And that something else stayed.

PART II — WHAT CAME BEFORE

Fear does not respect calendars. It moves forward and backward, returning long after the moment that first taught it how to live inside the body.

During the war, people spoke as if everything began in 1967, as if a date could contain what happened. But what I carried did not begin with bombs or uniforms. It began earlier, in the small changes adults made before anyone explained why those changes were necessary.

At the time, I could not have named it. I was young. I understood the world through details: voices lowered in mid-sentence, conversations that stopped when children entered the room, bags packed and unpacked as if repetition itself might prevent loss. These details were not trivial. They were warnings translated into daily life.

Adults tried to protect children by controlling what children knew. They replaced truth with reassurance. They said, "It will pass," because the alternative was unbearable. But children learn by watching what adults do when they think no one is watching.

That is how I learned the early signs of danger.

A family that keeps its bags close. A father who becomes absent without leaving. A mother who stops using full names in public. A household that avoids certain streets without explaining why.

During the war years, hunger and bombing took most of our attention. Survival leaves little room for reflection. But later, when the noise thinned, memory began to speak more clearly. It brought back the earlier fear—not as background, but as the beginning of the same story.

That is why I return to it here.

Because the war did not erase what came before. It carried it forward.

Violence announced itself first as rumor.

Before it arrived at the door, it moved through voices. People spoke in lowered tones, as if danger could hear its own name. News traveled without proof, and proof followed later, if it followed at all. In those days, certainty lagged behind fear.

I remember the way conversations changed shape. Adults leaned closer. Sentences ended early. Names were avoided. No one said exactly what was happening, but everyone adjusted as if they already knew.

Rumors arrived in clusters. Soldiers had taken power. Politicians were dead. The killings were targeted. Certain people should leave. Certain people should hide. No one could explain how to prepare for a threat that did not stay in one place.

What frightened me most was not what was said, but what followed the saying.

Mothers packed small bags and unpacked them again. Fathers stopped sleeping at home. Greetings shortened. Doors closed earlier. Children watched these changes closely, learning danger without being taught its language.

Warnings did not arrive as commands. No one said, Run now. Instead, people said, be careful, stay close, don't draw attention. Instructions were vague because the threat was vague.

Some rumors proved false. Others did not. The problem was that you could not tell the difference in time to act.

Rumors do not kill on their own. They prepare the ground.

By the time violence became visible, fear had already arrived.

The first flight did not feel like a decision. It felt like obedience to a new rule: do not wait.

By the time adults said we should prepare, preparation had already begun. Bags appeared in corners. Cloth was folded and refolded. Money was hidden in places children were not meant to notice. People stopped saying certain things out loud, as if words themselves could attract attention.

Rumors had done their work. They had trained everyone to expect violence without knowing its exact shape.

Then the shape arrived.

I remember movement more than beginnings. A house, a street, a familiar path—and then the knowledge that familiar no longer meant safe. Flight reduces life to what your hands can hold and what your feet can carry.

Later the distance would be measured as about 474 miles. At the time it was not miles. It was days and nights. It was forests and open fields. It was walking when the body wanted to stop, sometimes without water or food, because stopping felt like offering yourself to whoever might be searching.

We learned quickly that the safest roads were not always roads. We moved through trees because trees do not ask questions. We moved through shadows because shadows do not reveal names.

I remember running—urgent, blind, unheroic. Running until the lungs burned and the mind became blank and the body did what it needed to do.

Along the way, we met others whose faces carried the same decision. Families became clusters. Strangers became companions for an hour, a night, a few miles—then disappeared into the larger stream of movement.

Transport appeared like relief and risk at once. Trains that were meant for goods carried people pressed together. Lorries overflowed. People climbed onto anything that moved, not because they knew where it led, but because any movement felt better than stillness.

When the East finally came into reach, it did not feel like arrival. It felt like a different kind of crowd—rooms full, grief everywhere, stories heavy in the mouth.

People call it "the first flight" as if it ended when we crossed into the East. But it continued inside us—as a way of listening first, trusting last, and keeping the mind prepared to leave again.

That is what flight does. It does not only move you from place to place.

It changes the way you belong to the world.

Before there were uniforms to fear, there were faces.

I did not understand then how quickly recognition could turn against you. A neighbor's greeting could change its tone without changing its words. The street looked the same. The danger did not.

We were marked without being told we were marked.

Nothing announced the change. What changed was attention: the way people looked longer, the way questions were asked casually and then repeated, the way names were spoken and then avoided.

Being Igbo had once felt like background—something that belonged to family, language, custom. Then, without explanation, it became a risk.

I remember realizing that safety no longer depended on what you did, but on what you were. That realization does not arrive as a thought. It arrives as a tightening in the body, as the instinct to stay close to walls, as the decision not to answer too quickly.

Uniforms came later. Before them came the sorting.

Accent mattered. Name mattered. Where you came from mattered. Silence mattered. Everything that once helped people recognize you as a neighbor now helped them recognize you as something else.

Adults rehearsed invisibility. Children were coached on what not to say. Visits shortened. Routes changed. Explanations were rare, because explanation itself carried risk. Children were expected to understand without understanding.

The most frightening thing was how ordinary it all looked. The sorting did not begin with shouting. It began with routine—a question here, a look there, a delay that did not need to exist. By the time fear became explicit, it had already been practiced.

People began to disappear. Sometimes they were taken. Sometimes they simply did not return. Often, no one asked where they had gone. Silence wrapped itself around absence until absence felt expected.

What marked us was not an armband or a document. It was familiarity turned inward. The knowledge that those who could name you could also identify you.

Violence does not need weapons to begin. It only needs permission.

And permission had already been given.

By the time the pogroms arrived with their full force, they did not feel like a beginning.

They felt like an unveiling.

By the time the violence revealed itself fully, it did not feel sudden. It felt prepared.

After the sorting came the movement, and after the movement came the certainty that what had been whispered was now being acted upon. The streets did not change their shape, but they changed their meaning. Ordinary days became dangerous without announcing themselves as different.

The pogroms were not battles. There were no front lines, no clear beginning or end. There was only chaos entering places that had once felt familiar. Homes were no longer private. Shops were no longer neutral. The world became porous, and danger moved through it without resistance.

I remember running.

Not running toward anything—only away. The body understood before the mind could organize thought. Running became instinct, and instinct became instruction. I remember confusion and noise, and the way urgency erased everything except the need to keep moving.

I remember bodies on the road, not as images I want to hold onto, but as obstacles we stepped around because stopping meant dying. The road taught us that grief could be postponed, and that survival demanded attention before memory.

Movement gathered people the way fear gathers crowds. Families clung together. Strangers pressed close. Decisions were made quickly and forgotten just as quickly. There was no time to ask who you were traveling with, only whether they were moving in the same direction.

Transport appeared without ceremony. Trains that were meant for goods carried people—bodies packed into spaces not designed for them, dignity reduced to what could be preserved under pressure. Lorries overflowed with families who had lost everything except the will to live.

No one asked where these vehicles were going. Direction mattered less than escape. Any movement felt safer than stillness.

The pogroms taught us that safety could collapse without warning, and that silence did not guarantee survival. What had been whispered now spoke openly through action. The sorting that had begun quietly now moved with force.

When we finally reached the East, we thought we were safe.

Instead, we found a land overflowing with grief. Every family had a story. Every home was crowded. Rooms held more people than they were meant to hold, and each person carried a version of what had been left behind. Everyone was waiting—for justice, for protection, for something that might make sense of what had happened.

It was there that Biafra was born—not first as a nation, but as an idea shaped by necessity: that survival within what had existed before no longer felt possible. What had driven us to run now demanded an answer.

Later, people would argue about what to call what we lived through. They would debate definitions and intentions, as if naming were the same as understanding. But what I remember does not depend on argument.

I remember running.

I remember the trains.

I remember the lorries.

I remember reaching the East and realizing that arrival did not erase what had happened—it only gathered it in one place.

The pogroms did not feel like a beginning. They felt like the moment when what had been prepared finally showed itself.

And once shown, it could not be unseen.

PART III — WHAT FOLLOWED

22

When the war ended, it did not end inside us.

People speak of peace as if it arrives fully formed—an announcement, a date, a turning of a page. But after years that blurred together—after hunger became normal and loss became routine—peace felt less like a change and more like an unfamiliar quiet.

The guns fell silent. The body did not.

At first, everyone looked for signs that the world had truly changed. People waited for markets to become normal again, for roads to feel safe again, for sleep to return without interruption. They waited as if normal life might reappear the way water returns after drought.

But safety is not restored simply because fighting stops.

We returned to places that no longer belonged to the people we remembered. Some homes were gone. Some were occupied. Some stood in the same shape but felt altered, like a familiar face after grief has rewritten it. Even when a building remained, the sense of protection it once offered had been weakened.

Adults tried to rebuild routine. They swept. They repaired. They planted. They spoke of tomorrow with cautious hope, as if hope itself needed permission.

Children watched and learned a new kind of uncertainty: the uncertainty of "after."

In the war, fear had a clear cause. In the aftermath, fear became habit. A loud sound still lifted the heart. A sudden crowd still tightened the throat. Even laughter sometimes felt suspicious, as if joy might be punished for returning too soon.

People told us we were safe now. But safety is more than the absence of violence. It is the return of trust.

And trust was the last thing to come home.

Silence can be loud when you have lived inside noise for too long.

After the war, the world did not immediately become gentle. It became uncertain in a different way. The body did not understand peace as a gift. It treated peace as a pause that could end without warning.

There was relief in the simplest things: waking without the sky demanding interpretation, walking without scanning every sound for meaning, hearing a door close without the heart lifting in response. But relief was not the same as safety. Safety had to be rebuilt, and rebuilding required trust.

Trust was slow to return.

People spoke of "moving on" as if it were a place you could reach by choosing the right attitude. But moving on is not a road. It is a negotiation between memory and the present, and memory does not negotiate on command.

Ordinary life returned in fragments. Markets found their rhythm again. Roads began to carry more than fear. People repaired roofs and swept floors and planted small things as if planting could prove the future.

And still, something remained suspended.

Some carried loss openly. Others carried it in silence. The deepest grief was often the grief that had nowhere to go. It lived behind the eyes and surfaced in small moments—when a name was mentioned, when a smell returned, when a sound opened a door you had kept shut.

The war had ended, but the habits of war continued.

A sudden noise still brought the body to attention. A raised voice still tightened the chest. Even laughter sometimes felt unfamiliar, as if joy had become something you had to learn again.

People told stories carefully. Some stories were repeated until they became fixed. Other stories were avoided until avoidance became tradition. Children learned what could be spoken and what could not. In that way, silence became another inheritance.

When the guns fell silent, the silence did not erase what had happened. It only made space for what had been held back to speak.

And what spoke first was not explanation. It was memory.

What remained after the war was not only what could be seen.

There were visible losses—homes altered or gone, possessions reduced to what could be carried, families reshaped by absence. But the deeper residue was quieter. It lived in habits. It lived in reflexes. It lived in the way the body held itself, even when danger was no longer immediate.

We learned to live with what remained the way people learn to live with a scar: not by forgetting it is there, but by building a life that accommodates it.

Some remnants were practical. A tendency to save even when there was enough. A reluctance to waste, because waste had once been dangerous. A preference for keeping important things close, because important things had once been taken. These habits did not feel like choices. They felt like common sense, even when the world changed and common sense should have changed with it.

Other remnants were less visible but more persistent.

Vigilance is a difficult habit to unlearn. After years of listening for what might come next, the mind keeps listening even when there is nothing to hear. The body stays prepared. A sudden sound still arrives as a question. A silence still arrives as a warning. Peace requires a kind of trust, and trust is slow when you have learned how quickly the world can shift.

Sometimes I noticed how war had reorganized my idea of time.

Before, the future had felt open. After, the future felt conditional. Plans could be made, but they were held lightly. Certainty became something you admired in others, not something you assumed for yourself. When people spoke confidently about what would happen next year, next month, even next week, I wondered what kind of life had taught them that confidence.

Grief also remained, though it did not always have language.

In the immediate aftermath, there was too much to do to sit with loss. People rebuilt and moved and worked. They repaired what could be repaired. They tried to make daily life possible. But grief does not disappear when you are busy. It waits. It returns when the world becomes quiet enough to hear it.

It returned in unexpected ways: a familiar smell, a phrase overheard, a moment of laughter that suddenly turned heavy. It returned not as a single memory but as a texture—the awareness that something had been taken and could not be restored.

Some people carried their stories openly. Others carried them under silence. In many families, silence became a kind of protection, as if speaking might reopen what had been sealed. But silence has consequences. What is not spoken does not vanish; it changes shape. It passes through the house without being named. It becomes an inheritance.

I began to understand that survival is not only the act of staying alive. It is the long work of learning how to live afterward without letting the past dictate every movement. That work is uneven. Some days it feels possible. Other days the old instincts return, firm and unquestioned.

Living with what remained meant accepting that the war had not ended in one place and begun in another. It had seeped into the boundaries of ordinary life.

And yet, ordinary life did return.

Not as it had been, but as something rebuilt—quietly, imperfectly, with repairs that showed. The days learned to hold routines again. People learned to plant and harvest again.

Children learned to grow into adulthood carrying both what they remembered and what they were never told. The war left many things behind. What remained in me was not only pain.

It was also the knowledge that life can be rebuilt from fragments, and that endurance is not a single act. It is a practice.

Silence did not begin after the war. It became visible then.

In the years that followed, there were many things people did not say—not because they were forgotten, but because they were carried too carefully to be spoken aloud. Silence settled into households the way dust settles: gradually, invisibly, and everywhere.

At first, the silence felt protective.

Adults avoided certain names. They changed the subject when memories surfaced too close to the present. They spoke of survival without revisiting what survival had required. Children learned, without instruction, which questions were welcome and which questions should remain unasked.

Silence became a language.

It taught us what could be spoken in public and what belonged only to the private spaces of thought. It taught us that some truths were safer when carried alone. It taught us that remembering too openly could feel like inviting danger back into the room.

But silence does not erase memory. It reorganizes it.

What was not said did not disappear. It moved into gestures, habits, and assumptions. It shaped how people reacted to uncertainty, how they prepared for loss, how they trusted— or did not trust—the world around them.

Children absorbed this inheritance without being told its name.

We learned caution before we learned context. We learned restraint before we learned explanation. We learned that some histories lived beneath the surface of daily life, influencing decisions without announcing themselves as history.

As I grew older, I began to recognize the weight of what had been passed down quietly.

Silence had allowed people to rebuild without being consumed by grief. It had given families a way to move forward when language felt inadequate. But silence also carried costs. What is not spoken cannot be examined. What is not examined can return without warning.

I began to understand that silence can protect, but it can also postpone reckoning.

In some families, silence hardened into denial. In others, it softened into a shared understanding that did not require words. Both forms were attempts to live with what remained.

The inheritance of silence is complicated. It is neither purely harmful nor purely kind. It is a strategy born of survival, shaped by necessity, and passed forward without ceremony.

At times, I found myself repeating it—choosing quiet when speech felt too heavy, avoiding details when details seemed to ask for more than I could give. At other times, I resisted it, sensing that silence had done all it could do and that something else was required.

What I came to believe is this: silence can carry a people through the immediate aftermath of catastrophe, but it cannot be the final answer.

Eventually, memory asks to be acknowledged—not loudly, not violently, but honestly.

Breaking silence does not mean abandoning restraint. It means choosing clarity over avoidance, understanding over suppression, and responsibility over fear.

This book is not an attempt to shatter silence.

It is an attempt to translate it—carefully, deliberately— into something that can be carried without being hidden.

I remember not because the past demands it, but because the future does.

For a long time, remembering felt like a private obligation—something carried quietly, without witnesses. Memory lived in the body, in reflexes and habits, in the way attention sharpened at certain sounds or silences. It did not require language to exist.

But memory changes when it is carried across time.

As the years passed, I began to understand that forgetting is not neutral. What is forgotten does not disappear; it loosens its boundaries and returns without context. When violence is remembered only as rumor or argument, its human cost becomes abstract. When it is not remembered at all, it becomes repeatable.

I remember to give memory a shape that can be held without distortion.

This book is not an accusation. It is not an attempt to settle arguments or assign final blame. It is an act of witness— measured, deliberate, and rooted in lived experience. It asks the reader to see what happened without turning it into spectacle.

What I lived through did not belong only to me. It belonged to families who ran, to children who learned vigilance too early, to communities that discovered how quickly familiarity could become danger. Remembering honors that shared reality.

I remember because silence, while necessary at times, cannot be the final inheritance.

Silence carried us through the immediate aftermath. It allowed people to rebuild when language felt inadequate. But silence cannot teach. It cannot warn. It cannot prepare the next generation for the costs of indifference or the consequences of fractured belonging.

Memory, when carried responsibly, can.

Remembering does not mean living inside the past. It means refusing to let the past live invisibly inside the present. It means choosing clarity over avoidance and understanding over erasure.

I remember because survival alone is not enough.

Survival answers the question of whether a life continues. Memory answers the question of what that life means—to those who lived it, and to those who inherit its outcomes without having chosen its circumstances.

If this book has a purpose, it is this: to offer memory as a form of continuity, not as a wound. To show that witness can be steady rather than loud, and that testimony can preserve dignity rather than reopen harm.

I remember so that what happened is not reduced to argument or silence.

I remember so that the sky, once learned as a warning, can be seen again as something that does not always demand fear.

And I remember because the work of repair—personal, communal, and moral—begins with seeing clearly what was endured.

ACKNOWLEDGMENTS

I am grateful to my family and to all civilians whose experiences were never recorded. This book is written in their memory as much as my own.

SOURCE NOTES

This memoir is based on personal recollection and family testimony. Where possible, events have been cross-referenced with historical sources concerning the Biafran War (1967–1970).

Any errors are unintentional and remain the responsibility of the author.

www.ingramcontent.com/pod-product-compliance
Lightning Source LLC
Chambersburg PA
CBHW060230170726
48004CB00004BA/1499